volume 12

MEN / HOMBRES/ HOMMES / UOMINI / MÄNNER

195 hairstyles

195 estilos

195 styles de coiffures

195 acconciature

195 frisuren

HAIR'S HOW ®

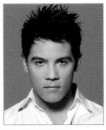

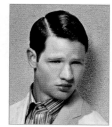

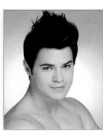
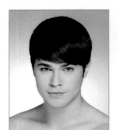

5

HAIR_ LEE MORAN FOR SANRIZZ
MAKEUP_ LEE PEARSON
STYLE_ VALENTINA TIURBINI
PHOTO_ ANDRES REYNAGA

HAIR_ LEE MORAN FOR SANRIZZ
MAKEUP_ LEE PEARSON
STYLE_ VALENTINA TIURBINI
PHOTO_ ANDRES REYNAGA

HAIR_ LEE MORAN FOR SANRIZZ
MAKEUP_ LEE PEARSON
STYLE_ VALENTINA TIURBINI
PHOTO_ ANDRES REYNAGA

HAIR_ LEE MORAN FOR SANRIZZ
MAKEUP_ LEE PEARSON
STYLE_ VALENTINA TIURBINI
PHOTO_ ANDRES REYNAGA

HAIR_ SAMUEL ROCHER
MAKEUP_ MOVIE
PHOTO_ PEDRO PACHECO
PRODUCTS_ DAVINES

HAIR_ SAMUEL ROCHER
MAKEUP_ MOVIE
PHOTO_ PEDRO PACHECO
PRODUCTS_ DAVINES

HAIR_ ALEXANDRE KIRILIUK @ SK STYLE BARCELONA
MAKEUP_ NATALIA SIDOROVA
PHOTO_ PAVEL OMELIUSIK

HAIR_ LUCIE SAINT-CLAIR
PHOTO_ RUDY WAKS

HAIR AND MAKEUP_ KAI UWE STEEG
PHOTO_ CARINA KOCH

HAIR AND MAKEUP_ KAI UWE STEEG
PHOTO_ CARINA KOCH

HAIR AND MAKEUP_ KAI UWE STEEG
PHOTO_ CARINA KOCH

HAIR_ WILLIAM DE RIDDER
STYLE_ VANKETS NICKY
PHOTO_ GHIELEN FRANK
PRODUCTS_ PAUL MITCHELL

HAIR_ GLENN VAN DIJKE AND CREATIVE TEAM KEUNE
MAKEUP_ DOMINIQUE SAMUELSEN
PHOTO_ HANS DE VRIES

HAIR_ AMY WOODS FOR TONI&GUY
CLOTHES_ REBECCA WHITE
PHOTO_ ZOE CALDWELL

HAIR_ AMY WOODS FOR TONI&GUY
CLOTHES_ REBECCA WHITE
PHOTO_ ZOE CALDWELL

HAIR_ AMY WOODS FOR TONI&GUY
CLOTHES_ REBECCA WHITE
PHOTO_ ZOE CALDWELL

HAIR_ AMY WOODS FOR TONI&GUY
CLOTHES_ REBECCA WHITE
PHOTO_ ZOE CALDWELL

HAIR_ GLENN VAN DIJKE AND CREATIVE TEAM KEUNE
MAKEUP_ DOMINIQUE SAMUELS
STYLE_ BONNIE ORLEANS VOSS
PHOTO_ HANS DE VRIES

HAIR_ MARK VAN WESTEROP @ KAPSALON SOLO
MAKEUP_ ANGELIQUE STAPELBROEK
STYLE_ PATRICIA GIESBERS
PHOTO_ HANS MOOIJER

HAIR_ MARK VAN WESTEROP @ KAPSALON SOLO
MAKEUP_ ANGELIQUE STAPELBROEK
STYLE_ PATRICIA GIESBERS
PHOTO_ HANS MOOIJER

HAIR_ MARK VAN WESTEROP @ KAPSALON SOLO
MAKEUP_ ANGELIQUE STAPELBROEK
STYLE_ PATRICIA GIESBERS
PHOTO_ HANS MOOIJER

HAIR_ MARK VAN WESTEROP @ KAPSALON SOLO
MAKEUP_ ANGELIQUE STAPELBROEK
STYLE_ PATRICIA GIESBERS
PHOTO_ HANS MOOIJER

HAIR AND MAKEUP_ TOM|CO. CREATIVE TEAM
CREATIVE DIRECTOR_ THOMAS-ARMIN MATHES
PHOTO_ DANIEL LUKAC FOR H7 PHOTO
DIGITAL ARTWORK_ ANN CHRISTIN SCHUHMACHER FOR PUSH THE BUTTON

HAIR AND MAKEUP_ TOM | CO. CREATIVE TEAM
CREATIVE DIRECTOR_ THOMAS-ARMIN MATHES
PHOTO_ DANIEL LUKAC FOR H7 PHOTO
DIGITAL ARTWORK_ ANN CHRISTIN SCHUHMACHER FOR PUSH THE BUTTON

HAIR_ HAIR MACHINE

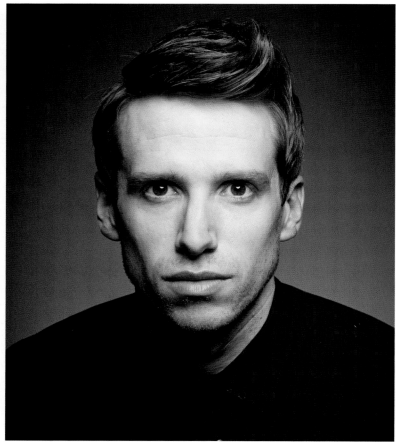

HAIR_ HAIR MACHINE

HAIR_ HAIR MACHINE

HAIR_ HAIR MACHINE

HAIR_ HAIR MACHINE

HAIR_ HAIR MACHINE

HAIR_ HAIR MACHINE

HAIR_ HAIR MACHINE

HAIR_ HAIR MACHINE

HAIR_ HAIR MACHINE

HAIR_ HAIR MACHINE

HAIR_ HAIR MACHINE

HAIR_ HAIR MACHINE

HAIR_ HAIR MACHINE

HAIR_ HAIR MACHINE

HAIR_ HAIR MACHINE

ART-DIRECTOR_ WILLIAM LEPEC FOR INTERMÈDE
MAKEUP_ VESNA ESTORD
STYLE_ KATHRIN LEZINSKY
PHOTO_ OLIVIER BRAUMANN

ART-DIRECTOR_ WILLIAM LEPEC FOR INTERMÈDE
MAKEUP_ VESNA ESTORD
STYLE_ KATHRIN LEZINSKY
PHOTO_ OLIVIER BRAUMANN

HAIR_ MICHEL DERVYN ARTISTIC TEAM
PHOTO_ LAURENCE LABORIE

HAIR_ SAMUEL ROCHER, SEIHA PON, MÓNICA DIAS, CRISTIANO NAPOLITANO @ LEO COSTA
MAKEUP_ TÂNIA CARVALHO ASSISTED BY CÁTIA MENDES @ ATELIER DO CHIADO
PHOTO_ PEDRO PACHECO
PRODUCTS_ DAVINES & MOVIE

HAIR_ SAMUEL ROCHER, SEIHA PON, MÓNICA DIAS, CRISTIANO NAPOLITANO @ LEO COSTA
MAKEUP_ TÂNIA CARVALHO ASSISTED BY CÁTIA MENDES @ ATELIER DO CHIADO
PHOTO_ PEDRO PACHECO
PRODUCTS_ DAVINES & MOVIE

ART-DIRECTOR_ FABIEN PROVOST FOR FRANCK PROVOST
MAKEUP_ C. WILLER
PHOTO_ A. AWAD

HAIR_ STEVN THOMAS, CREATIVE DIRECTOR JAM TEAM
MAKEUP_ BIG LIDIA
STYLE_ NILA AGENCY MILAN
PHOTO_ STEVN THOMAS

HAIR_ STEVN THOMAS, CREATIVE DIRECTOR JAM TEAM
MAKEUP_ BIG LIDIA
STYLE_ NILA AGENCY MILAN
PHOTO_ STEVN THOMAS

HAIR_ SHARON COX AND LEONARDO RIZZO
MAKEUP_ LEE PEARSON
STYLE_ VALENTINI TIURBINI
PHOTO_ ANDRES REYNAGA

HAIR_ SHARON COX AND LEONARDO RIZZO
MAKEUP_ LEE PEARSON
STYLE_ VALENTINI TIURBINI
PHOTO_ ANDRES REYNAGA

HAIR_ SHARON COX AND LEONARDO RIZZO
MAKEUP_ LEE PEARSON
STYLE_ VALENTINI TIURBINI
PHOTO_ ANDRES REYNAGA

HAIR_ SHARON COX AND LEONARDO RIZZO
MAKEUP_ LEE PEARSON
STYLE_ VALENTINI TIURBINI
PHOTO_ ANDRES REYNAGA

HAIR_ RUDY PIGNATARO @ SALON G&A
PHOTO_ DAVID HOU

HAIR_ RUDY PIGNATARO @ SALON G&A
PHOTO_ DAVID HOU

HAIR_ RUDY PIGNATARO @ SALON G&A
PHOTO_ DAVID HOU

HAIR_ STUDIO CHIRIK

HAIR_ SHAMPOO ARTISTIC TEAM
PHOTO_ LAURENCE LABORIE

HAIR_ CEBADO

HAIR_ CEBADO

ART DIRECTION_ GARY FRANCE, SACHA MASCOLO-TARBUCK & COS SAKKAS
HAIR_ JIM SHAW @ ESSENSUALS MEN
STYLE_ URSULA LAKE
MAKEUP_ HIROMI UEDA
PHOTO_ ANDREW O'TOOLE

HAIR_ LEE MORAN FOR SANRIZZ
MAKEUP_ KASIA DZIADEL
STYLE_ ELIZA HEINEZEN
PHOTO_ ANDRES REYNAGA

HAIR_ LEE MORAN FOR SANRIZZ
MAKEUP_ KASIA DZIADEL
STYLE_ ELIZA HEINEZEN
PHOTO_ ANDRES REYNAGA

HAIR_ LEE MORAN FOR SANRIZZ
MAKEUP_ KASIA DZIADEL
STYLE_ ELIZA HEINEZEN
PHOTO_ ANDRES REYNAGA

CREATIVE DIRECTOR_ NORA BORDJAH FOR JEAN LOUIS DAVID
HAIR_ JEFF CAUSSE AND VIRGINIE MESSAI
MAKEUP_ DELPHINE EHRHART
DESIGN_ NICOLAS VALOTEAU
PHOTO_ DEREK KETTELA

ART-DIRECTOR_ WILLIAM LEPEC FOR INTERMÈDE
MAKEUP_ JOELLE GARNERET
STYLE_ MICHELLE ANANOU
PHOTO_ RICHARD ZOUARI

HAIR_ MICHEL DERVYN ARTISTIC TEAM
PHOTO_ LAURENCE LABORIE

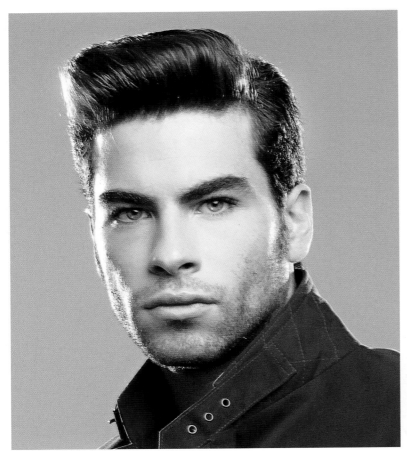

HAIR_ MADRIGAL

HAIR_ MADRIGAL

HAIR_ MADRIGAL

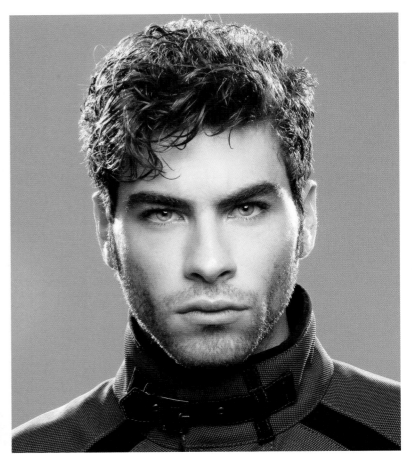

HAIR_ MADRIGAL

HAIR_ MADRIGAL

HAIR_ HAIR MACHINE

HAIR_ HAIR MACHINE

HAIR_ HAIR MACHINE

HAIR_ HAIR MACHINE

HAIR_ HAIR MACHINE

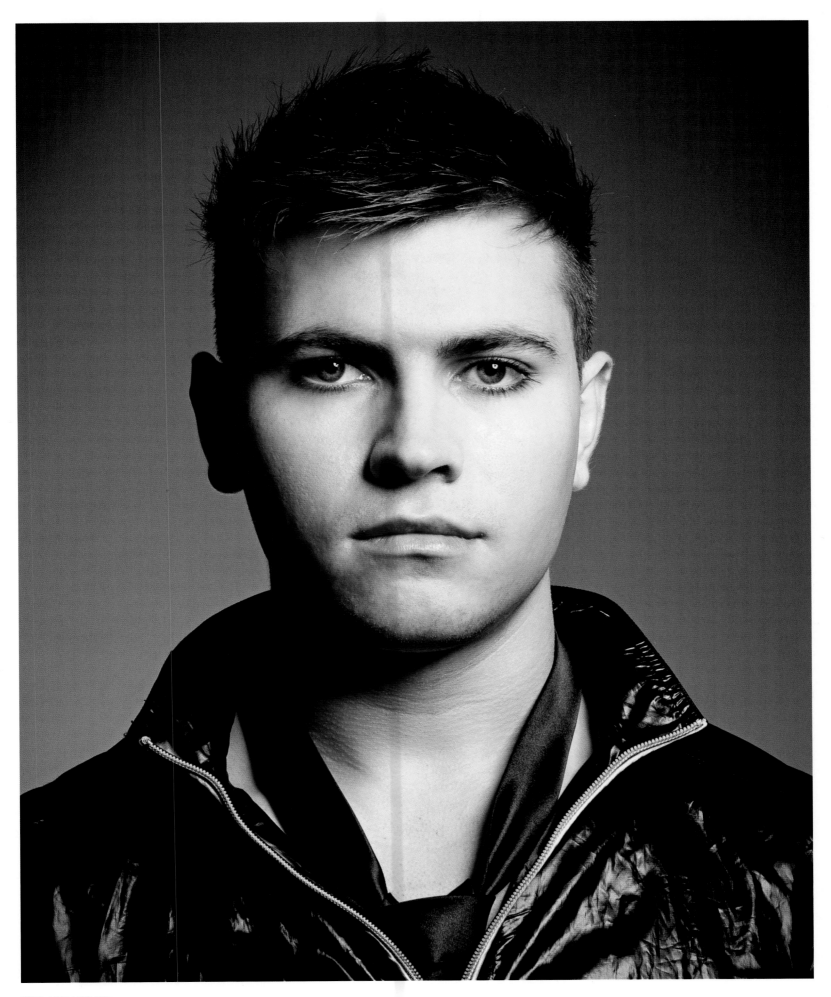

HAIR_ HAIR MACHINE

HAIR_ NATALIA YAVORSKAIA FOR SALERM COSMETICS
MAKEUP_ IRINA OJERELIEVA
CLOTHES_ YURI STAVTSEV
MODEL_ ANDREY MATIUSHENKO
PHOTO_ ANDREY MIKHEEV

HAIR_ NATALIA YAVORSKAIA FOR SALERM COSMETICS
MAKEUP_ IRINA OJERELIEVA
CLOTHES_ YURI STAVTSEV
MODEL_ ANDREY MATIUSHENKO
PHOTO_ ANDREY MIKHEEV

HAIR AND STYLE_ CATALAN PERRUQUERS
PHOTO_ EDU GARCIA

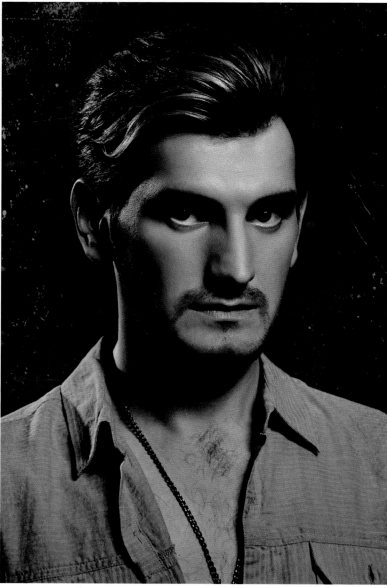

HAIR_ SVETLANA KUZNETSOVA, OLGA JIGATCHEVA, VLADIMIR GASKOV FOR HAIR CLUB
MODEL_ IGNAT ABDULAEV, ULTRA MODELS
PRODUCTS_ REVLON PROFESSIONAL

HAIR_ SVETLANA KUZNETSOVA, ANNA CHUSOVA, YULIA MURATOVA FOR HAIR CLUB
MODEL_ OLEG MALISHEV, ULTRA MODELS
PRODUCTS_ REVLON PROFESSIONAL

HAIR_ SVETLANA KUZNETSOVA, ALEXANDRE GAZIZOV, MARINA ZEIBERT FOR HAIR CLUB
MODEL_ MARCUS NERIUS, ULTRA MODELS
PRODUCTS_ REVLON PROFESSIONAL

HAIR_ FABIO MESSINA FOR DIADEMA
MAKEUP_ CRISTINA MARZO FOR 20100MILANO
PHOTO_ STEFANO BIDINI

HAIR_ FABIO MESSINA FOR DIADEMA
MAKEUP_ CRISTINA MARZO FOR 20100MILANO
PHOTO_ STEFANO BIDINI

HAIR_ FABIO MESSINA FOR DIADEMA
MAKEUP_ CRISTINA MARZO FOR 20100MILANO
PHOTO_ STEFANO BIDINI

HAIR_ FABIO MESSINA FOR DIADEMA
MAKEUP_ CRISTINA MARZO FOR 20100MILANO
PHOTO_ STEFANO BIDINI

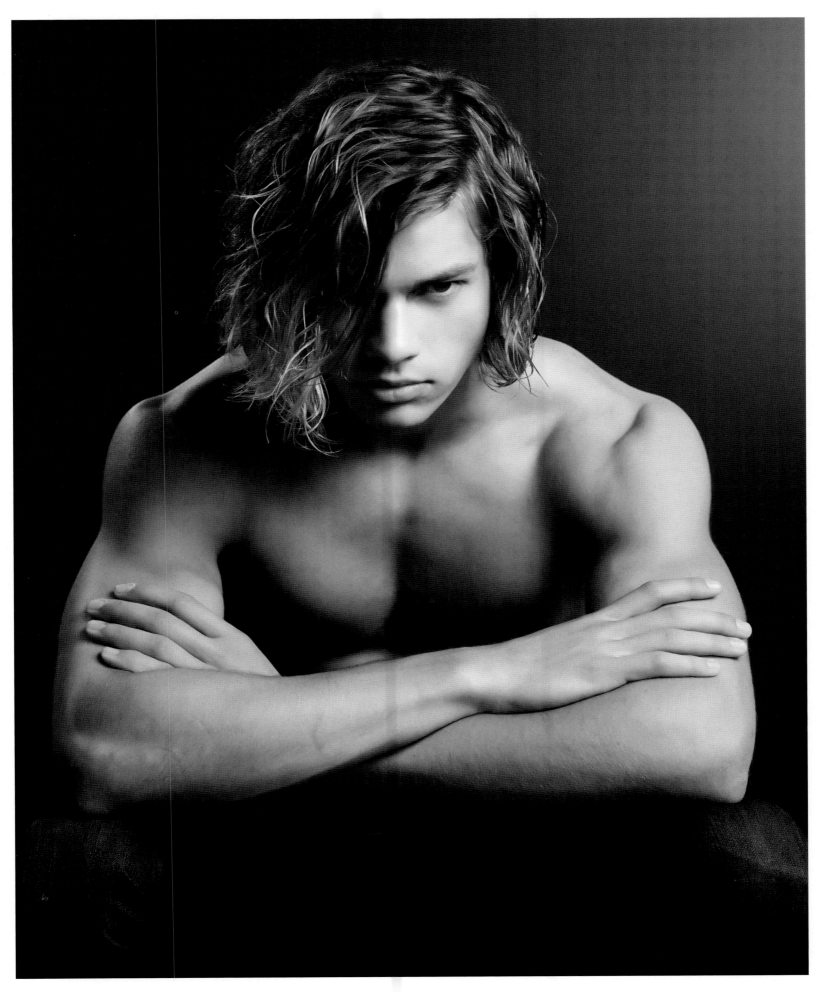

HAIR_ FABIO MESSINA FOR DIADEMA
MAKEUP_ CRISTINA MARZO FOR 20100MILANO
PHOTO_ STEFANO BIDINI

HAIR_ FABIO MESSINA FOR DIADEMA
MAKEUP_ CRISTINA MARZO FOR 20100MILANO
PHOTO_ STEFANO BIDINI

HAIR_ FABIO MESSINA FOR DIADEMA
MAKEUP_ CRISTINA MARZO FOR 20100MILANO
PHOTO_ STEFANO BIDINI

HAIR_ FABIO MESSINA FOR DIADEMA
MAKEUP_ CRISTINA MARZO FOR 20100MILANO
PHOTO_ STEFANO BIDINI

HAIR_ FABIO MESSINA FOR DIADEMA
MAKEUP_ CRISTINA MARZO FOR 20100MILANO
PHOTO_ STEFANO BIDINI

HAIR_ FABIO MESSINA FOR DIADEMA
MAKEUP_ CRISTINA MARZO FOR 20100MILANO
PHOTO_ STEFANO BIDINI

HAIR_ FABIO MESSINA FOR DIADEMA
MAKEUP_ CRISTINA MARZO FOR 20100MILANO
PHOTO_ STEFANO BIDINI

HAIR_ FABIO MESSINA FOR DIADEMA
MAKEUP_ CRISTINA MARZO FOR 20100MILANO
PHOTO_ STEFANO BIDINI

HAIR_ FABIO MESSINA FOR DIADEMA
MAKEUP_ CRISTINA MARZO FOR 20100MILANO
PHOTO_ STEFANO BIDINI

HAIR_ FABIO MESSINA FOR DIADEMA
MAKEUP_ CRISTINA MARZO FOR 20100MILANO
PHOTO_ STEFANO BIDINI

HAIR_ FABIO MESSINA FOR DIADEMA
MAKEUP_ CRISTINA MARZO FOR 20100MILANO
PHOTO_ STEFANO BIDINI

 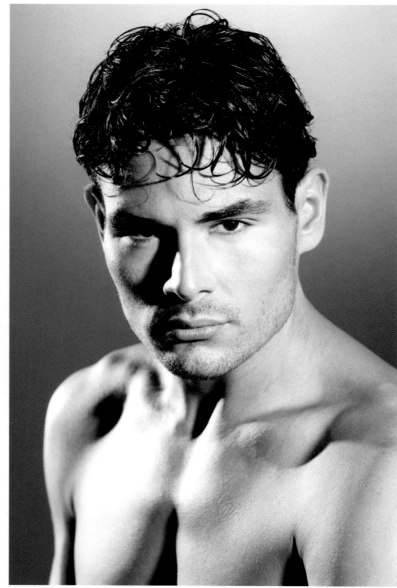

ART-DIRECTOR_ FABIO MESSINA
HAIR_ DIADEMA FOR X-MEN
MAKEUP_ CRISTINA MARZO FOR 20100MILANO
PHOTO_ STEFANO BIDINI

ART-DIRECTOR_ FABIO MESSINA
HAIR_ DIADEMA FOR X-MEN
MAKEUP_ CRISTINA MARZO FOR 20100MILANO
PHOTO_ STEFANO BIDINI

ART-DIRECTOR_ FABIO MESSINA
HAIR_ DIADEMA FOR X-MEN
MAKEUP_ CRISTINA MARZO FOR 20100MILANO
PHOTO_ STEFANO BIDINI

ART-DIRECTOR_ FABIO MESSINA
HAIR_ DIADEMA FOR X-MEN
MAKEUP_ CRISTINA MARZO FOR 20100MILANO
PHOTO_ STEFANO BIDINI

ART-DIRECTOR_ FABIO MESSINA
HAIR_ DIADEMA FOR X-MEN
MAKEUP_ CRISTINA MARZO FOR 20100MILANO
PHOTO_ STEFANO BIDINI

ART-DIRECTOR_ FABIO MESSINA
HAIR_ DIADEMA FOR X-MEN
MAKEUP_ CRISTINA MARZO FOR 20100MILANO
PHOTO_ STEFANO BIDINI

ART-DIRECTOR_ FABIO MESSINA
HAIR_ DIADEMA FOR X-MEN
MAKEUP_ CRISTINA MARZO FOR 20100MILANO
PHOTO_ STEFANO BIDINI

ART-DIRECTOR_ FABIO MESSINA
HAIR_ DIADEMA FOR X-MEN
MAKEUP_ CRISTINA MARZO FOR 20100MILANO
PHOTO_ STEFANO BIDINI

ART-DIRECTOR_ FABIO MESSINA
HAIR_ DIADEMA FOR X-MEN
MAKEUP_ CRISTINA MARZO FOR 20100MILANO
PHOTO_ STEFANO BIDINI

ART-DIRECTOR_ FABIO MESSINA
HAIR_ DIADEMA FOR X-MEN
MAKEUP_ CRISTINA MARZO FOR 20100MILANO
PHOTO_ STEFANO BIDINI

ART-DIRECTOR_ FABIO MESSINA
HAIR_ DIADEMA FOR X-MEN
MAKEUP_ CRISTINA MARZO FOR 20100MILANO
PHOTO_ STEFANO BIDINI

ART-DIRECTOR_ FABIO MESSINA
HAIR_ DIADEMA FOR X-MEN
MAKEUP_ CRISTINA MARZO FOR 20100MILANO
PHOTO_ STEFANO BIDINI

ART-DIRECTOR_ FABIO MESSINA
HAIR_ DIADEMA FOR X-MEN
MAKEUP_ CRISTINA MARZO FOR 20100MILANO
PHOTO_ STEFANO BIDINI

HAIR_ DMITRY SHEPELENKO FOR OLEXANDER SITNIKOV SALON
MAKEUP_ DMITRY SHEPELENKO
PHOTO_ ALEXANDRE IZOTOVS

HAIR_ LARISA SKRIPNIK FOR OLEXANDER SITNIKOV SALON
MAKEUP_ DMITRY SHEPELENKO
PHOTO_ ALEXANDRE IZOTOVS

HAIR_ EDOUARD FEDORENKO FOR OLEXANDER SITNIKOV SALON
MAKEUP_ DMITRY SHEPELENKO
PHOTO_ ALEXANDRE IZOTOVS

HAIR_ ALEXEI KRIVORUCHKO FOR OLEXANDER SITNIKOV SALON
MAKEUP_ DMITRY SHEPELENKO
PHOTO_ ALEXANDRE IZOTOVS

HAIR_ HARM-JAN STOUWDAM @ SALON B
PHOTO_ ARMANDO BRANCO

HAIR AND STYLE_ RUSTAM MIRASOV

HAIR AND STYLE_ RUSTAM MIRASOV

ART-DIRECTOR_ DENIS CHIRKOV
HAIR_ GALINA ONISCHENKO, NATALIA OROPAI FOR ESTEL PROFESSIONAL
MAKEUP_ DARIA STAKHOVSKAIA
PHOTO_ IGOR SAKHAROV, ANTON MILLER

HAIR_ HAIR MACHINE

HAIR_ GLENN VAN DIJKE AND CREATIVE TEAM KEUNE
MAKEUP_ DOMINIQUE SAMUELS
STYLE_ BONNIE ORLEANS VOSS
PHOTO_ HANS DE VRIES

HAIR_ JAMIE STEVENS @ ERROL DOUGLAS
MAKEUP_ MIA WILKHOLM
STYLE_ GOK WAN
PHOTO_ JENS WILKHOLM
PRODUCTS_ MATRIX

HAIR_ JAMIE STEVENS @ ERROL DOUGLAS
MAKEUP_ MIA WILKHOLM
STYLE_ GOK WAN
PHOTO_ JENS WILKHOLM
PRODUCTS_ MATRIX

HAIR_ JAMIE STEVENS @ ERROL DOUGLAS
MAKEUP_ MIA WILKHOLM
STYLE_ GOK WAN
PHOTO_ JENS WILKHOLM
PRODUCTS_ MATRIX

HAIR_ PAUL WILSON & THERI DEJOODE FOR AMERICAN CREW
MAKEUP_ SAMANTHA TRINH
CLOTHES_ JAMES WORTHINGTON DEMOLET
PHOTO_ DAVID RACCUGLIA, AMERICAN CREW FOUNDER AND CREATIVE DIRECTOR

78

HAIR_ LISA MUSCAT @ E SALON
MAKEUP_ VICTORIA BARRON
STYLE_ PETA-MARIE RIXON
PHOTO_ PAUL SCALA

HAIR AND MAKEUP_ KAI UWE STEEG
PHOTO_ CARINA KOCH

HAIR AND MAKEUP_ KAI UWE STEEG
PHOTO_ CARINA KOCH

HAIR AND MAKEUP_ KAI UWE STEEG
PHOTO_ CARINA KOCH

HAIR AND MAKEUP_ KAI UWE STEEG
PHOTO_ CARINA KOCH

HAIR_ NICK IRWIN AND ANTHONY MASCOLO @ TIGI INTERNATIONAL CREATIVE TEAM

MAKEUP_ PAT MASCOLO, AMY BARRINGTON AND JOSE BASS

PHOTO_ ANTHONY MASCOLO AND ROBERT AGUILAR

PRODUCTS_ TIGI BED HEAD

HAIR_ DESMOND MURRAY
MAKEUP_ JO SUGAR
STYLE_ KARL WILLETT
PHOTO_ DESMOND MURRAY

HAIR_ DESMOND MURRAY
MAKEUP_ JO SUGAR
STYLE_ KARL WILLETT
PHOTO_ DESMOND MURRAY

HAIR_ DESMOND MURRAY
MAKEUP_ JO SUGAR
STYLE_ KARL WILLETT
PHOTO_ DESMOND MURRAY

HAIR_ DESMOND MURRAY
MAKEUP_ JO SUGAR
STYLE_ KARL WILLETT
PHOTO_ DESMOND MURRAY

HAIR_ DESMOND MURRAY
MAKEUP_ JO SUGAR
STYLE_ KARL WILLETT
PHOTO_ DESMOND MURRAY

HAIR_ DESMOND MURRAY
MAKEUP_ JO SUGAR
STYLE_ KARL WILLETT
PHOTO_ DESMOND MURRAY

HAIR_ DESMOND MURRAY FOR GOLDWELL
MAKEUP_ JO SUGAR
STYLE_ SOBHON MCDONAGH
PHOTO_ DESMOND MURRAY

HAIR_ DESMOND MURRAY FOR GOLDWELL
MAKEUP_ JO SUGAR
STYLE_ SOBHON MCDONAGH
PHOTO_ DESMOND MURRAY

HAIR_ DESMOND MURRAY FOR GOLDWELL
MAKEUP_ JO SUGAR
STYLE_ SOBHON MCDONAGH
PHOTO_ DESMOND MURRAY

HAIR_ SHAMPOO ARTISTIC TEAM
PHOTO_ LAURENCE LABORIE

HAIR_ SHAMPOO ARTISTIC TEAM
PHOTO_ LAURENCE LABORIE

HAIR_ DENIS CHIRKOV FOR ESTEL PROFESSIONAL
MAKEUP_ DARIA STAKHOVSKAIA
PHOTO_ GOSHA SEMENOV

HAIR_ DENIS CHIRKOV FOR ESTEL PROFESSIONAL
MAKEUP_ DARIA STAKHOVSKAIA
PHOTO_ GOSHA SEMENOV

HAIR_ DENIS CHIRKOV FOR ESTEL PROFESSIONAL
MAKEUP_ DARIA STAKHOVSKAIA
PHOTO_ GOSHA SEMENOV

HAIR_ THOMAS SCHUNG, KELLER THE SCHOOL CREATIVE TEAM
MAKEUP_ TINKA LUPTAKOVA
CLOTHES_ FRANK OBERBERGER
PHOTO_ VLADO GOLUB

HAIR_ THOMAS SCHUNG, KELLER THE SCHOOL CREATIVE TEAM
MAKEUP_ TINKA LUPTAKOVA
CLOTHES_ FRANK OBERBERGER
PHOTO_ VLADO GOLUB

HAIR_ J.7 ARTISTIC TEAM
MAKEUP_ ELENA HERLET
DESIGN_ ENGENHART STUTTGART*BERLIN
PHOTO_ VLADO GOLUB

HAIR_ J.7 ARTISTIC TEAM
MAKEUP_ ELENA HERLET
DESIGN_ ENGENHART STUTTGART*BERLIN
PHOTO_ VLADO GOLUB

HAIR_ J.7 ARTISTIC TEAM
MAKEUP_ ELENA HERLET
DESIGN_ ENGENHART STUTTGART*BERLIN
PHOTO_ VLADO GOLUB

HAIR_ KARINE JACKSON
MAKEUP_ MARGARET ASTON
STYLE_ LETICIA DARE
PHOTO_ ANDREW O'TOOLE
PRODUCTS_ ORGANIC COLOUR SYSTEMS

HAIR_ KARINE JACKSON
MAKEUP_ MARGARET ASTON
STYLE_ LETICIA DARE
PHOTO_ ANDREW O'TOOLE
PRODUCTS_ ORGANIC COLOUR SYSTEMS

HAIR_ KARINE JACKSON
MAKEUP_ MARGARET ASTON
STYLE_ LETICIA DARE
PHOTO_ ANDREW O'TOOLE
PRODUCTS_ ORGANIC COLOUR SYSTEMS

HAIR_ KARINE JACKSON
MAKEUP_ MARGARET ASTON
STYLE_ LETICIA DARE
PHOTO_ ANDREW O'TOOLE
PRODUCTS_ ORGANIC COLOUR SYSTEMS

HAIR_ KARINE JACKSON
MAKEUP_ MARGARET ASTON
STYLE_ LETICIA DARE
PHOTO_ ANDREW O'TOOLE
PRODUCTS_ ORGANIC COLOUR SYSTEMS

HAIR_ KARINE JACKSON
MAKEUP_ MARGARET ASTON
STYLE_ LETICIA DARE
PHOTO_ ANDREW O'TOOLE
PRODUCTS_ ORGANIC COLOUR SYSTEMS

HAIR_ STEVN THOMAS, CREATIVE DIRECTOR JAM TEAM
MAKEUP_ LEA DELUCA
PHOTO_ STEVN THOMAS
PRODUCTS_ HAIRCONCEPT

HAIR_ STEVN THOMAS, CREATIVE DIRECTOR JAM TEAM
MAKEUP_ LEA DELUCA
PHOTO_ STEVN THOMAS
PRODUCTS_ HAIRCONCEPT

HAIR_ CEBADO

HAIR_ AMERICAN CREW ARTISTIC TEAM **ART-DIRECTOR_** PAUL WILSON
MAKEUP_ SAMANTHA TRINH
STYLE_ JAMES WORTHINGTON
PHOTO_ TIM TUCKER

HAIR_ HAIR MACHINE

HAIR_ HAIR MACHINE

HAIR_ HAIR MACHINE

HAIR_ VITALY BODROV FOR OV SALON   **HAIR_** VITALY BODROV FOR OV SALON

HAIR AND MAKEUP_ RAFFEL PAGES
PHOTO_ SERGI JASANADA

HAIR, STYLE AND MAKEUP_ RUSTAM MIRASOV
PHOTO_ SERGEY LEGAREV

HAIR, STYLE AND MAKEUP_ RUSTAM MIRASOV
PHOTO_ SERGEY LEGAREV

HAIR, STYLE AND MAKEUP_ RUSTAM MIRASOV
PHOTO_ SERGEY LEGAREV

HAIR_ ANDRIUS MASAUSKAS & ANATOLIJUS PAJANOK @ CREATIVE TEAM A••TWINS
MAKEUP_ INGUTÈ KSIVICKIENÈ, ALA VOLKOVA @ ANDRÈ TEAM
PHOTO_ DARIUS TARELA

HAIR_ ANDRIUS MASAUSKAS & ANATOLIJUS PAJANOK @ CREATIVE TEAM A••TWINS
MAKEUP_ INGUTÈ KSIVICKIENÈ, ALA VOLKOVA @ ANDRÈ TEAM
PHOTO_ DARIUS TARELA

HAIR_ ANDRIUS MASAUSKAS & ANATOLIJUS PAJANOK @ CREATIVE TEAM A••TWINS
MAKEUP_ INGUTÈ KSIVICKIENÈ, ALA VOLKOVA @ ANDRÈ TEAM
PHOTO_ DARIUS TARELA

ART-DIRECTOR_ NORA BORDJAH FOR JEAN LOUIS DAVID
HAIR_ MAX LAFFITTE & JEFF CAUSSE
MAKEUP_ DELPHINE ERHARD
DESIGN_ POLEY LUARD **PHOTO_** DEREK KETTELA

ART-DIRECTOR_ NORA BORDJAH FOR JEAN LOUIS DAVID
HAIR_ MAX LAFFITTE & JEFF CAUSSE
MAKEUP_ DELPHINE ERHARD
DESIGN_ POLEY LUARD **PHOTO_** DEREK KETTELA

ART-DIRECTOR_ BETTI BONGIASCA
HAIR_ ITALIAN STYLE FRAMESI
MAKEUP_ SILVIA DELL'ORTO
STYLE_ EVELYN EFFRIM BOTCHEY
PHOTO_ FABIO COSTI

HAIR_ STUDIO CHIRIK

HAIR_ JEAN VALLON
MAKEUP_ KARINE
STYLE_ JEAN VALLON
PHOTO_ MARIO SINISTAJ

HAIR_ ROBERT STARY
MAKEUP_ FILIP NOVAK
STYLE_ EVA BRZAKOVA
PHOTO_ NICOLA FRAJEROVA

HAIR_ ROBERT STARY
MAKEUP_ FILIP NOVAK
STYLE_ EVA BRZAKOVA
PHOTO_ NICOLA FRAJEROVA

HAIR_ ROBERT STARY
MAKEUP_ FILIP NOVAK
STYLE_ EVA BRZAKOVA
PHOTO_ NICOLA FRAJEROVA

HAIR_ BARBARA WUILLOT
PHOTO_ MARIUS BARAGAN

HAIR_ BARBARA WUILLOT
PHOTO_ MARIUS BARAGAN

HAIR_ BARBARA WUILLOT
PHOTO_ MARIUS BARAGAN

HAIR_ BARBARA WUILLOT
PHOTO_ MARIUS BARAGAN

HAIR, MAKEUP AND STYLE_ ACADEMY AGILIER FOR KEUNE HAIRCOSMETICS
CLOTHES_ MAX CHERNITSOV
ASSISTANT PHOTO AND MAKE_ ALEXEI DROZZIN
PHOTO_ DMITRY BOCHAROV

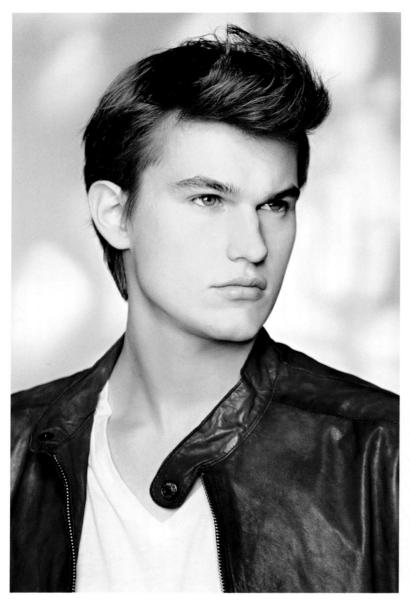

HAIR_ CEBADO

HAIR_ SEMION AVANESOV, SALON FUKKO
PHOTO_ IGOR MAIATSKY

ART-DIRECTOR_ FABIEN PROVOST FOR FRANCK PROVOST
MAKEUP_ C. WILLER
STYLE_ F. BLANC
PHOTO_ A. AWAD

ART-DIRECTOR_ WILLIAM LEPEC FOR COIFF&CO
MAKEUP_ VESNA ESTORD
STYLE_ KATHRIN LEZINSKY
PHOTO_ NICOLAS BUISSON

ART-DIRECTOR_ WILLIAM LEPEC FOR COIFF&CO
MAKEUP_ VESNA ESTORD
STYLE_ KATHRIN LEZINSKY
PHOTO_ NICOLAS BUISSON

HAIR_ MOVING HAIR ARTISTIC TEAM

HAIR_ MOVING HAIR ARTISTIC TEAM

ART-DIRECTOR_ CATHY MONNIER FOR SAINT ALGUE
MAKEUP_ L. DROUEN
STYLE_ A. TESSON
PHOTO_ G.-M. ZIMMERMAN

Volume 12 / Volumen 12/ Volume 12/ Volume 12/ Band 12

MEN / HOMBRES/ HOMMES / UOMINI / MÄNNER

Published by / Publicado por / Publié par/ Pubblicato da / Herausgegeben von

HAIR'S HOW
5645 Coral Ridge Drive # 131
Coral Springs, FL 33076, USA
Ph. 1-954-323-8590, Fax 1-951-344-2240
e-mail: publisher@hairshow.us

Distributed by / Distribuido por / Distribué par/ Distribuito da / Vertrieben von

HAIR'S HOW
5645 Coral Ridge Drive # 131
Coral Springs, FL 33076, USA
Ph. 1-954-323-8590, Fax 1-951-344-2240
www.hairshow.us, e-mail: sales@hairshow.us

Exclusive distributor in Canada/Distribudor exclusivo en Canada/
Distributeur exclusif en Canada/ Distributore esclusivo in Canada/
Exklusive Vertriebsgesellschaft in Kanada:
Novostyl International, 3152 Joseph-Monier, Terrebonne, QC J6X 4R1, CANADA,
Ph. 1-800-465-9247, www.novostyl.com, e-mail: printing@novostyl.com

HAIR'S HOW Vol. 12: MEN
HAIR'S HOW, VOLUME 12: HOMBRES
HAIR'S HOW, VOLUME 12 : HOMMES
HAIR'S HOW, VOLUME 12: UOMINI
HAIR'S HOW, BAND 12: MÄNNER

ISBN 978-0-9822037-5-0

Printed in EU / Impreso en EU / Imprimé en Europe/Stampato in EU / Gedruckt in der EU

First edition / Primera edición / Première edition/ Prima edizione/ Erste Auflage